Three Dogs, Two Mules, and a Reindeer

True Animal Adventures on the Alaska Frontier

Three Dogs, Two Mules, and a Reindeer

True Animal Adventures on the Alaska Frontier

Marjorie Cochrane

Illustrated by Jon Van Zyle

2010

Mountain Press Publishing Company

Missoula, Montana

Library of Congress Cataloging-in-Publication Data

Cochrane, Marjorie.
  Three dogs, two mules, and a reindeer : true animal adventures on the
Alaska frontier / Marjorie Cochrane ; illustrated by Jon Van Zyle.
     p. cm.
  Includes bibliographical references and index.
  ISBN 978-0-87842-564-8 (pbk. : alk. paper)
  1. Animals—Alaska—Anecdotes. 2. Natural history—Alaska—
Anecdotes. I. Van Zyle, Jon, ill.   II. Title.
  QL161.C63 2010
  636.009798—dc22

                    2009034530

PRINTED IN HONG KONG

MP Mountain Press
PUBLISHING COMPANY
P.O. Box 2399 · Missoula, MT 59806 · 406-728-1900
800-234-5308 · info@mtnpress.com
www.mountain-press.com

To Byron

Table of Contents

Acknowledgments

I could not ask for a better editor than Gwen McKenna. She not only made many improvements to my manuscript, but double-checked historical facts and was open to my suggestions as well. Jon Van Zyle's artwork is a major contribution, and designer Jeannie Painter has put everything together beautifully. I also owe thanks to former members of the Alaska State Historical Commission and to newspaper editor Lee Jordan for introducing me many years ago to Alaskan history and encouraging me to write about it. My children continue to be enthusiastic critics and supporters.

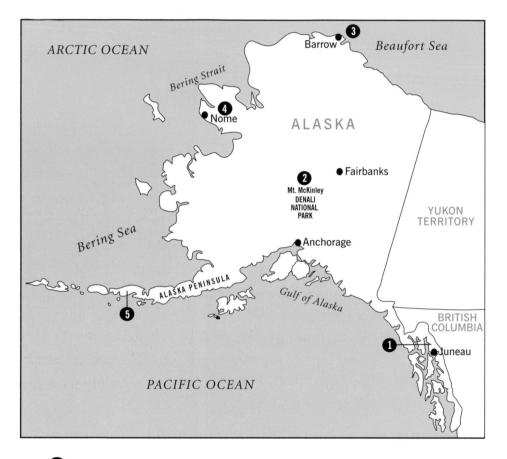

ARCTIC OCEAN

Beaufort Sea

Barrow ③

Bering Strait

ALASKA

④ Nome

② ● Fairbanks

Mt. McKinley
DENALI
NATIONAL
PARK

YUKON
TERRITORY

Bering Sea

● Anchorage

ALASKA PENINSULA

⑤

Gulf of Alaska

BRITISH
COLUMBIA

① ● Juneau

PACIFIC OCEAN

① John Muir and Stickeen

② James Wickersham and the mules

③ Vilhjalmur Stefansson and Bones

④ Tautuk and Dynamite

⑤ Bernard Hubbard and Margie

Introduction

If you board an Alaska-bound plane from the "lower forty-eight," you'll be soaring over "the Last Frontier" in only a few hours. Flying over jagged peaks and glacial snowfields, bays, and rivers, you'll see few signs of towns or roads. The landscape would have looked much the same a hundred years ago, but the same journey—by ship or kayak—took weeks or months.

The stories in this book took place from the 1880s to the 1930s, times when few people knew much about Alaska. They are about explorers who wanted to find out more about "the Great Land," which is what the word *Alaska* means in the language of the native Aleut people. But these stories are also about animals who accompanied the human adventurers across glaciers, tundra, and icy waters and helped make their journeys possible.

Each of these true stories occurred in a different part of Alaska. Stickeen's adventure with John Muir took place in southeastern Alaska, the long narrow strip of land bordered by Canada on one side and the Pacific Ocean on the other. In south-central Alaska, where more than half of the state's population now lives, two mules named Mark and Hannah helped James Wickersham's expedition explore Mt. McKinley. "Bones" occurred in the northwestern Arctic, the true land of the midnight sun. "Dynamite and the Reindeer Fair" happened on the Seward Peninsula, which touches the Bering Strait. Finally, you'll meet Margie and her puppies in southwestern Alaska, the region that includes the Aleutian Islands, which stretch nearly to Russia.

So put on your parka and pack up your gear. Through the words and pictures on these pages, we can travel back in time and join these intrepid people and animals on their extraordinary adventures.

Stickeen, the Dog Who Explored Glaciers

OHN MUIR hadn't wanted the odd little dog, Stickeen, to follow him on his exploration that stormy morning. He and his fellow explorers had been awakened often during the night by the shriek of wind in the spruces. It would not be easy going for a small dog. But as Muir, up before daylight, set out alone to explore the icy landform he called the Taylor Bay glacier, now known as Brady Glacier, on the southeast coastline of Alaska, he found Stickeen following at his heels. "Go back!" Muir commanded the raggedy mongrel. "Go back where you'll be warm and safe, and where breakfast awaits."

But the dog would not obey. Finally Muir gave in. "Come then, if you must," he sighed. He broke off a piece of the bread he had put in his pocket for lunch and gave it to his little companion, a short-legged black mutt with a bushy tail. Off the pair went into the gathering storm.

John Muir in Alaska, examining a spruce bough, 1879
—Courtesy Alaska State Library Photograph Collection, John Muir-2

Stickeen wasn't Muir's dog. He belonged to Rev. S. Hall Young and his wife. Young was part of Muir's Alaska expedition of 1880. The explorers had paddled up the coast with Tlingit Indian guides to study the glaciers of the new territory. During the journey, Stickeen adopted Muir as his special friend. He sat under Muir's legs in the long Tlingit canoe, and at night he slept at his feet. This expedition was one of many for John Muir, who explored countless acres of wilderness in the western United States and dedicated much of his life to helping conserve wild places. On this trip, the little black dog had accompanied him wherever he went.

Earlier in the journey, on a warm, sunny day, Stickeen had trotted for thirty miles beside Muir across a frozen glacial lake. The ice was honeycombed and sharp. Before long, Stickeen's feet were cut and bleeding, but he wouldn't turn back. Taking pity on his companion, Muir used his handkerchiefs to fashion little moccasins for Stickeen's paws.

Now on this cold, blustery morning in late August, Muir and Stickeen climbed steadily through the woods that bordered the edge of the glacier. By midmorning they were crossing the treacherous snow and ice of the glacier itself. The wind blew sheets of rain and swirls of mist across their path. Muir bent his head against the force of the storm. But the weather didn't bother Stickeen. He ran happily back and forth.

In spite of the cold and sleet, Muir often paused to relish the beautiful, pure blue of the ice or to watch and listen to a silvery stream rushing by. The pair reached the other side of the glacier safely, but Muir did not have time to explore. "Come, Stickeen," he said. "It's nearly five o'clock and we have fifteen miles to go to reach camp and our good warm dinners."

Once he was out of sight of the woods, Muir used his compass to find his way back over the glacier's ice fields. He and Stickeen were nearly across when Muir found himself in a maze of crevasses—wide, deep cracks in the ice. Some were narrow enough to be jumped, while others had to be crossed on natural ice bridges. As they neared the end of the maze, they came to a crevasse that was about eight feet wide—a very long jump for Muir. Beyond it, the ice appeared smooth and even, so the explorer decided to take the risk. Gathering all his strength, he leaped across, barely making it. Small though he was, Stickeen jumped the chasm as if it were nothing.

Past this hurdle, Muir found to his dismay that their troubles were far from over. He and the dog had mistakenly jumped onto an island of ice, which was a few hundred yards wide and about two miles long. After a brief search, Muir realized that the only way to get off the island was to cross the narrowest, most treacherous ice bridge he had ever seen. The bridge was a jagged sliver that spanned the fifty-foot crevasse in a low, drooping curve, starting eight to ten feet below where Muir and Stickeen stood. To reach it, Muir would have to cut footholds into the steep frozen wall of the crevasse with his ax and climb down. If he slipped, he could easily plunge to his death. But he had no other choice. Darkness was coming fast, and with no food and no protection from the storm, Muir could not risk being trapped on the glacier overnight.

Already cold, wet, hungry, and tired, Muir leaned down and set to work on the daunting operation. He took out his small ax, reached down over the side of the crevasse, and began to carve ice steps and finger holds into the cliff. As Muir worked, Stickeen crept along the edge, peering down into the chasm. He laid his head on Muir's shoulder and looked at him as if to say, "Surely you're not going down there!" It was the first sign of fear Muir had ever seen in the scrappy little dog.

As he finished each foothold and hand notch, Muir cautiously climbed farther down into the crevasse. With each new step, he leaned down, perilously, to chop out the next one. When he finally reached the edge of the ice bridge,

he chipped out a small platform to land on. There he adjusted himself into position. Straddling the knifelike edge of the ice bridge, he worked his way across inch by inch. As he went, he shaved off the sharp top of the ice to form a narrow but flat surface for Stickeen to walk on. At the far side, Muir chipped out another platform and again cut steps and finger holds to climb up. At last, he was at the top and safe.

All the while, Stickeen had been running nervously back and forth on the other side of the crevasse. To reach Muir, he would have to climb down a nearly vertical wall of ice to reach the ice bridge, then cross the bridge on the path Muir had carved for him, which was barely four inches wide, and finally, climb back up another sheer ice wall. The little dog began to whimper, seeming to sense that of all his adventures, never before had he been in so dangerous a situation. Could he do it?

"Come, wee laddie! You won't fall," Muir called encouragingly. But Stickeen's crying became more intense. His unshakable courage seemed to have left him. He stood and howled in utter despair.

Muir agonized. With night approaching, he could not afford to wait long for his canine friend. Would he have to abandon the little fellow after all? "Stickeen! I must go on. You can come if you try."

Suddenly, Stickeen fell silent and crept forward to the edge of the crevasse. Crouching low, he slid down the treacherous cliff to the first foothold. He worked his way down, step by step, the same way, until he reached the bottom and the start of the ice bridge. Now he inched out onto the sliver of ice. Snow was falling and the wind threatened to blow him into the abyss below. He moved slowly and deliberately, his claws gripping the ice. Finally, miraculously, he was across!

But he was not safe yet. He still had an obstacle to overcome, perhaps the hardest one of all—climbing up the second cliff. He halted and looked up at the ice steps, as if to assess the situation and plan a strategy. Suddenly, he leapt up, scrambling up the footholds so quickly that Muir was not sure how he did it.

Now on the level surface where Muir stood, Stickeen ran around in elated circles. "Well done, little boy!" Muir cried, relieved and delighted. The explorer tried to catch him to hug him and pet him, but Stickeen kept running back and forth and round and round, barking in hysterical joy. Just as Muir thought the dog had exhausted himself, Stickeen dashed madly away, then turned and made a running leap into Muir's arms, nearly knocking him over. Then off he darted again.

Muir knew they still had many miles to go. He started walking, knowing Stickeen would follow. They would be traveling in the dark, but the terrain was safe now. When the two cold and weary adventurers finally reached camp, Rev. Young and the Tlingit guides had a fire blazing and a hot meal waiting. Muir and Stickeen were too exhausted to eat much, though. They were even too exhausted to sleep well. "Both of us," Muir wrote in his journal, "fancied we were still on that dreadful ice bridge in the shadow of death."

But the next morning, Muir's agitation gave way to joy at being alive. "Never before had rocks and ice and trees seemed so beautiful and wonderful," Muir marveled as the expedition party paddled away to the next destination. "Even the cold biting rainstorm . . . seemed wonderful compensation for all that we had endured, and we sailed down the bay through the gray, driving rain, rejoicing."

After the expedition was over, Muir never saw Stickeen again. A few years later, he learned that the dog was stolen from Rev. Young and carried off on a steamboat. "His fate is wrapped in mystery," Muir noted sadly.

Before his death in 1914, John Muir explored many remote and beautiful areas of the western United States. He identified flowers and trees, probed unknown mountains and forests, and recommended ways to conserve them. At his urging, Congress set aside 148 million acres of national forests and established Yosemite National Park in California. But his happiest memories were of his Alaskan travels, when the glacial ice was smooth and blue, and the little dog Stickeen ran excitedly beside him.

◇◇◇◇◇◇◇◇◇◇◇◇◇◇◇◇◇◇◇◇◇◇

The silky-haired little dog who became Muir's companion had arrived in Wrangell as a puppy, carried in the pocket of Muir's friend and travel companion, Rev. S. Hall Young. Although he was unlike their own larger hunting dogs, the Stikine Tlingits, who lived on the Stikine River in southeastern Alaska, found the pup so clever and humorous that they adopted and named him—an exceptional honor, Rev. Young said. In the Tlingit language, *stikine* means "great." In Muir's time, the name was spelled *Stickeen*.

The Stikine River delta is a stopover on the Pacific Flyway for shorebirds, snow geese, sandhill cranes, and bald eagles. When the spring run of eulachon, more commonly called hooligan or smelt, reaches the delta in late April, the largest concentration of bald eagles in North America arrives to feast on them.

Dinnaji, the
White Man's Moose

THE TENA ATHAPASKAN INDIAN children jumped with excitement on the banks of the Kantishna River, in the great Tanana Valley in interior Alaska. They laughed and pointed at the steamboat, the *Tanana Chief*. It was like no boat the children had ever seen. No one was paddling it. Smoke rose from a large pipe in the middle of it. Strangest of all, it carried some sort of moose on board.

"Dinnaji, *dinnaji!*" the children exclaimed, their word for moose. These animals were smaller than the moose they knew, and they had no antlers, but the color of their hides and the shape of their ears resembled a moose, the animal that provided the Athapaskans with food and clothing. The men on the steamboat were white, so the Tena children called the peculiar beasts "white man's *dinnaji*—white man's moose."

The animals were not moose, but mules. Their names were Mark and Hannah, and they were the first mules ever to arrive in the Tanana Valley. The animals had spent the winter hauling supplies from the goldfields of the Yukon in Canada to the new gold town of Fairbanks, Alaska. Now, in May 1903, they were on loan to James Wickersham, judge for the third judicial district of Alaska, to help him on his expedition to climb Mt. McKinley, the highest peak in North America. Wrote Wickersham, "They were the only mules to be had in the Tanana valley and were, of course, gladly accepted." He knew he was lucky to get them. "They were thoroughbred Kentucky mules, young and strong, yet learned in the ways of pack-saddles and mountain trails."

A pack train of mules hauling supplies in the Yukon Territory, sometime between 1896 and 1913
—Courtesy Anchorage Museum at Rasmuson Center, John Urban Collection, AMRC-b64-1-90

Accompanying Wickersham on board the *Tanana Chief* were George Jeffrey, Mort Stevens, interpreter John McLeod, and mule packer Charlie Webb. They wanted to be the first men to reach the top of the great mountain. The Indians called the peak *Denali*, which in the Athapaskan language means "the high one." Judge Wickersham thought it was too bad that the United States had chosen to officially name the mountain after a president instead of adopting its beautiful Indian name.

The Tena children and adults watched with interest as the mules were led on the shore, where the expedition party's long overland journey would begin. The Indians' dogs barked and nipped at the legs of the strange new creatures. Mark and Hannah were good-tempered mules, but the noisy crowd was upsetting. Mark tucked his head, lifted his hind legs, and kicked at the dogs. The Tenas laughed, but they also recognized the power of the mules' hooves and moved back.

The Tenas turned to the white men, eager to find out what they were doing in this part of Alaska. When interpreter McLeod described the expedition's plans, the Indians were bewildered. Denali was too steep to climb. "Mountain sheep fall off that mountain," they said. "Are you looking for gold?"

"No, not for gold," Wickersham replied. "We are going merely to see the top, to be the first to reach its summit."

The Tenas laughed. "You are a fool," they said. Foolish though it might have seemed to the Indians, it had been the judge's dream to climb the great Denali ever since he arrived in Alaska three years before. Now he finally had the time to do it.

Wickersham asked if the Indians would help him find the base of the mountain. The old hunters, who were acquainted with the caribou hills near Denali, drew maps with charcoal on birch bark to show the route. A

Judge James Wickersham in Alaska, near Denali, 1903
—Courtesy Alaska State Library, Wickersham State Historic Sites Photograph Collection, P277-018-043

younger Indian offered to guide them as far as the summer hunting grounds of Koonah, a blind Athapaskan chief.

Wickersham's men had found an abandoned boat in the river and decided to use it for hauling some of the expedition's supplies. The party split up. "Webb, McLeod, and I will go with the boat," Wickersham noted, "while Jeffrey and Stevens will go overland with the mules and meet us at old Koonah's camp."

After a three-day journey, Wickersham's group found Koonah's people camped on an island in the Kantishna River, which was running high from the spring snowmelt. Jeffery and Stevens had also reached the river, but they had not crossed over to the island because the mules had refused to put their hooves into the icy stream. Some of the men proceeded to Koonah's camp, leaving the problem of the skittish Mark and Hannah for the morning.

The next day, the explorers went back to take the mules, "much against their will," across the river. "We first led Hannah gently to the high bank above the wide rolling torrent and kindly invited her to enter and swim as if it were an ordinary everyday matter," Wickersham wrote. But she backed away, shaking her big ears as if to say "No!" They tugged at her reins and pleaded with her in cajoling voices. "Be nice, old girl, it's all right," Jeffrey urged, to no avail. Finally, Webb tied one rope behind Hannah's rump and another around her neck, then he tied the ropes to Wickersham's boat. Then, with "a most unsportsmanlike kick," he shoved Hannah over the bank and into the river, where the others towed her across. After that, they went back and towed Mark to the island the same way, much to the amusement of the Tenas watching from the shore. As the explorers dragged the chagrined and bedraggled mules into the village, the Indians and their dogs, Wickersham wrote, "howled in happy unison at the first circus perfomance ever exhibited in Tenaland."

Athapaskan woman at her camp with sleeping baby and dogs, 1902
—Courtesy Anchorage Museum at Rasmuson Center, Crary-Henderson Collection, AMRC-b62-1-571

The river island where Koonah's people were camped lay in a wide, forested valley, where streams descended from the foothills of Denali. Glistening high above was the massive dome of the mountain. That evening, as men rested on spruce boughs and the campfire flickered in the half-darkness of the Alaskan spring night, old Koonah told them legends of the Tena people. He told them of Yako, a mighty Tena magician, and how he created the great mountain called Denali.

"Long ago," Koonah began, "Yako dwelt in the land where the Tena live. He was young and strong and as straight and tall as a spruce tree growing by the river. He was as gentle as a young caribou, as strong as a bull moose, as wise as the beaver."

Yako had no wife and greatly desired one, but there were no women among the Tenas. To find one, he had to travel to the village of the mighty hunter Totson, the war chief of the Raven tribe. Yako made a birchbark canoe and "launched it on the waters of the Yukon and floated upon its swift current to the great saltwater, and paddled across the summer sea to sunset land where lived the Raven chief." As he approached the Raven village, he sang, "Oh, mighty Totson, chief of the Raven tribe, hunter of men and animals, I ask you for a beautiful female to be my wife."

But Totson, who was jealous of Yako's youth and power, refused to hear his song. He sat in his underground house sharpening a magic war spear to kill him. Totson's wife, however, heard the song and brought her beautiful daughter, Tsukala, to Yako, urging him to flee with her.

Yako hid Tsukala in his canoe under a blanket of white sheep's wool and paddled swiftly away. Totson was furious and "caused a storm to rise and great green waves to roll, and, armed with his mighty spear, pursued Yako over the wild sea waves. Putting forth all his skill and strength, Totson prepared to kill him with one mighty thrust of his great war spear."

But Yako saw the spear in the air and "bringing his most powerful magic force to his aid, he changed a giant wave into a mountain of stone." The spear glanced harmlessly off the wall of the great stone mountain. Totson's canoe crashed into the mountainside, and he was thrown upon the rocks. There he transformed into a large black raven.

"That mountain," Koonah said, "is now called Denali, the High One." The water path that Yako followed is now the valley of the Yukon and Tanana

Rivers, he explained, home to the Tena, the descendants of Yako the magician and his wife Tsukala. "Totson the Raven has killed neither man nor animal since that fateful day. He caws repeatedly, begging Yako to change him back into a man and warrior. But no answer has ever come."

When Koonah ended his tale, the explorers sat quietly gazing at the dusky midnight light shimmmering on the great mountain of the legend. Would they be the first to reach its peak?

The next morning, May 24, the explorers said goodbye to Koonah and his people and set out for the long journey over the Chitsia Hills to Denali's base. Beautiful sunny days alternated with miserably cold and wet ones. Traveling through forests of birch and spruce, they often had to cut trails with their axes. Many creeks had to be carefully forded. The mules became tired and sore, and Mark developed a bad lesion on his back from the packsaddle. On June 7, as the party struggled over broken rocks in search of a campsite, the mules bolted into a narrow gorge. It took the men hours to catch them, and it was midnight before they could make camp.

In mid-June the party reached the high meadows of caribou country, on Denali's northern slopes. It was a hunter's paradise, as Judge Wickersham called it. One afternoon, when Mark and Hannah were turned loose to graze, an inquisitive herd of caribou trotted over to inspect the mules. "Their friendly curiosity cost one his life, for Webb shot it to replenish our larder with fresh steaks."

Before beginning their climb, the explorers stopped to cut wood, which they would need to carry for camping above the timberline. Then the mules, their packs loaded with the wood and supplies, followed the men to the base of mountain walls, which rose almost 15,000 feet to the peak.

As the expedition began the ascent, the men found that great avalanches of melting snow and ice roared down on them during the day. To avoid the problem, Wickersham and his companions suspended their climb until late in the evening, when the sun's warmth had left the slopes. There would be no safe footing for the mules, so they were left at the base camp with McLeod. Each man carried a knapsack filled with enough dried caribou meat, bread, and chocolate to last three or four days, in case they were detained. They were equipped with ropes and alpenstocks—long staffs with a pointed iron tip on one end and a sharp-edged pick on the other.

To reach the ridge that they thought would lead to the summit, the explorers had to cross a dangerous ice field filled with crevasses and seemingly bottomless pits. Great towers of ice hovered overhead. The men climbed steadily through the summer-lit night. The leader tapped the ground ahead with his alpenstock to test the snow's surface for hidden crevasses. They walked fifty feet apart; this way, if one person fell into a crevasse, he would not pull the others in with him, and they would be able to pull him out. Sometimes they encountered ice bridges so narrow that they had to cross them on their hands and knees.

By early morning, the climbers saw that they were near the ridge. But to their disappointment, they found that the route they had chosen ended in an almost perpendicular cliff—it did not connect with the summit ridge. Here, at 10,000 feet—halfway to the top—there was no way they could continue. "Reluctantly," Wickersham wrote in his journal, "we recognize that we are inviting destruction by staying here and we have concluded that there is no possible chance of further ascent from this side of Denali."

Saddened but persevering, they retraced their steps to the base camp. Maybe they could try again. They could go farther around the base of the mountain, perhaps, and try another route. But it was no use. They did not have enough food left to try a different route, and the snowfields, softened by

the sun of midsummer, were becoming more dangerous each day. They had no choice but to go home.

To return to the Tanana River, where they would catch a steamboat home, the explorers built a raft to carry them down the Kantishna. Early in the trip, however, the raft capsized, and the party lost most of its remaining supplies. The men continued downstream on foot. The riverbank was treacherous—muddy and full of quicksand. "Our mules are constantly sinking into dangerous quicksands. Both mules mired to exhaustion today and we saved them from being actually engulfed in quicksand only by thrusting small logs under them as they floundered and by assisting them with ropes."

Having little food left, the explorers lived for days on bannocks, a kind of biscuit, which the men made by mixing flour with glacial water and baking it on flat rocks by the campfire. When Wickersham noticed dark brown spots in his bannock and remarked that they looked like currants, Webb exclaimed, "Hah, them's mosquitoes!"

"We ate pounds of [mosquitoes] in our bannocks," Wickersham recalled. "I've disliked . . . currant cake ever since that experience."

By the end of June, the flour was nearly gone and the party's only other provision was half a handful of salt. One day, when the men went out to hunt moose, Hannah found the salt and ate it, sack and all. Now the men would not even have the pleasure of seasoning for their meat.

Upon reaching the gentler lower stretches of the Kantishna, the company built another raft, which they steered with a long pole. This one had an enclosure for Mark and Hannah. Now they could "take our entire party aboard and float with the current, which is now placid but strong enough to carry us downstream about three miles an hour."

The weather was mild, and the party floated smoothly downstream. The men slept on the raft, stopping to go ashore only long enough to cook their food and let Mark and Hannah graze. "[The mules] jump off the raft when we stop to cook, and fill their stomachs with lush grasses while we rest; then [they] march down and jump on the raft, where they stand as gently beside the pole as if they had always traveled on rafts," Wickersham wrote.

Free from the flies and mosquitoes which had plagued them on land, the men relaxed and the mules slept long hours. By the Fourth of July the trip was nearly over. The men celebrated the holiday by firing a volley of shots from their guns. The noise, Wickersham said, "almost caused Hannah to jump overboard."

When the expedition reached the Tanana River, at the mouth of the Kantishna, the men put Mark and Hannah aboard the steamer *North Star* to return them to their owners in Fairbanks. The mules were plump and healthy, in better condition, Wickersham pointed out, than when they had started on their journey two months earlier. Little did they know the important part they had just played in the first attempt to scale the mighty Denali.

Although he had not reached the top, Wickersham looked on the bright side. For him and his companions, the effort to climb North America's highest peak had been an adventure worth having:

> We returned . . . without any feeling of failure but with a glow of satisfaction that we had done so much with so little. . . . We blazed the trail to the great mountain's northern base, mapped its approaches, the trails and rivers. . . . We passed two happy months wandering as freely and happily as our brothers the Tena hunters. During our too brief time in this unexplored wilderness we stood with bared heads before the crystal throne of Yako, the mighty Tena magician, and gazed with awe upon the stupendous creations of ice and snow which adorn it. We surveyed its greatest glacier, climbed halfway to its summit. . . . No lover of nature, of mountains, glaciers, and high places, can have any sense of defeat after such a journey and we felt none.

◇◇◇◇◇◇◇◇◇◇◇◇◇◇◇◇◇◇◇◇◇◇◇◇

Twenty-one-year-old Walter Harper, a native Alaskan, became the first person to set foot on the south summit of Mt. McKinley, its highest point. He was a member of a four-man climbing team led by Episcopalian Archdeacon Hudson Stuck, with companions Harry Karstens and Robert Tatum. It had taken the men nearly a month of climbing from their base camp to reach the mountain's top on June 7, 1913. They calculated its height as 20,320 feet, making it the highest peak in North America.

The men had ordered the best mountaineering equipment they could buy from the East Coast. But when the shipment arrived, on the last boat of the season, they were dismayed to find that all of their special alpine boots were too small. They made their climb in moccasins worn over five pairs of wool socks. Also missing from the shipment were their new tents, so the team had to rely on an old tent for their base camp, and they made their own smaller ones for the climb.

The climbing party left Nenana on March 17 with two dog teams to transport their supplies, traveling some 150 miles to the base camp. An Athapaskan teenager, fifteen-year-old Johnny Fred, stayed at the base camp with the dogs while the others made the ascent. The climbers were gone nearly two weeks longer than they had expected, but Johnny kept the dogs well fed by hunting mountain sheep and caribou, saving his own ration of sugar and canned milk for the men when they returned.

The Arctic Adventures of Bones the Sled Dog

A CRACKLING SOUND coming from beyond the ice floe awakened the sled dog called Bones. He tilted his head and pointed his ears toward the sound, trying to identify it. It was softer than the familiar sound of ice floes grinding against each other—this was something he hadn't heard before.

Bones and five other sled dogs were tied to toggles fastened into the ice. Nearby was a tent where three men lay sleeping, members of a small Arctic expedition studying ocean currents in the Beaufort Sea, north of the Alaska and Canadian mainland.

Bones wiggled as close to the sound as the rope would let him get. It seemed to be coming from under the lead, the open water between the ice floes. During the night, the lead had frozen over with six inches of new ice. Now Bones saw that the lead ice was bulging and cracking. The crackling noise was followed a moment later by a hiss and a column of spray as a great beluga whale broke through the ice, leaping into the air. Then it crashed back through the lead ice and disappeared.

Bones barked with excitement. The other dogs, awakened by the commotion, joined the barking. Also awakened were the three men, who sprang from their tent to see what was happening as several more whales pushed through the ice and swam by.

"The belugas are back!" exclaimed Storker Storkerson.

"As sure a sign of spring as anyone could wish for," his friend Ole Andreasen said with a smile.

But the sight of the whales worried Vilhjalmur Stefansson, the leader of the expedition. Warmer weather meant less ice and more open water between them and the shore. The men could not cross deep water on their sleds, so if too much ice melted, they would not be able to get back to Banks Island, still several hundred miles away, in time to catch their boat home. If they missed the rendezvous, they would have to spend another winter out on the ice.

The explorers, who had started their expedition near the Alaska-Canada border in March of 1914, were trying to find out if any undiscovered land still lay in this little-known part of the Arctic. Stefansson also wanted to prove that humans could live on what nature provided, even on polar ice. For almost two months, the ice had been home to the men and their dogs. They had started with a load of 1,236 pounds of food, fuel, hunting gear, scientific instruments, and miscellaneous supplies, which the dogs hauled on heavy sleds. When the provisions ran out, the men hunted seals, using the animals' blubber for both food and fuel.

"The dogs are rested and well-fed," Stefansson wrote in his journal. "If we have water-sky today we must look for a way to cross the lead." During

Sleds used on the Stefansson expedition of 1913–14 —Courtesy Library of Congress

his many years in the north, Stefansson had learned about water-sky from the Inuit Eskimos. They showed him that when solid gray clouds covered the sky, the sky could serve as a mirror. Dark strips of open water would be reflected as black lines on the gray above, whereas over ice, the sky would be white. This sky map would show the explorers which way to travel to avoid open water.

"Bones will pull well, now that his stomach is full of seal meat," Storkerson said. Hearing his name, Bones thumped his bushy gray-and-white tail enthusiastically on the ice. Of all the dogs, he was the plumpest. Even when the food was running low, Bones's frame remained well covered with a layer of fat. Thus the men jokingly called him "Bones."

Like the other dogs, Bones had lived all his life in the Arctic. He was part Eskimo dog, part mastiff, part St. Bernard, and part wolf. Mixed-breed dogs, Stefansson felt, had a sense of duty and a willingness to work even when they were tired and hungry. But Bones seemed to be the exception. When he was hungry, he saved his strength by slackening on the straps,

Vilhjalmur Stefansson, 1912 —Courtesy Library of Congress

called traces, that tied him to the other dogs on the team, forcing them to pull his share of the load. Neither did Bones like to exert himself when he was warm and comfortable. "He seems to lack character," Stefansson observed with displeasure. Few people would put up with a lazy dog on their team. But Stefansson felt that Bones was useful as long as he was well fed, and besides, his antics amused the men.

Early in the journey, Bones had narrowly escaped drowning. A gale wind and thick flying snow had forced the men to camp on ice that was cracking and breaking as the wind pushed floe against floe. Late in the night, the howls of a dog awakened Storkerson. Hurrying out, he found that the ice where Bones was tied was breaking away from the campsite, and the dog was being dragged into a slowly opening channel of icy water. Pushing with his haunches, Bones pulled hard against the rope, but he was sliding closer and closer to the widening lead.

Storkerson quickly unfastened the rope and pulled Bones to safety. Figuring the crisis was over, Storkerson turned to go back to his sleeping bag when he saw a huge ice ridge, fifteen feet high, looming behind the men's tent. The ridge had formed during the night from the high winds. Now, only a little more movement could send huge ice chunks tumbling down onto the camp. Storkerson awakened the other men, and they hastily loaded their sled, hitched the dogs, and moved to a safer spot to wait out the storm. Though Storkerson had saved Bones's life that night, Bones, unknowingly, may also have saved him and his companions. Upon hearing how the men came to be warned of the danger, Andreasen remarked, "Perhaps that lazy Bones is good for something after all."

Not long afterward, it was Stefansson's turn to rescue Bones, this time from a polar bear. Scouting for a route through the leads and ice mush,

the explorers were perhaps a quarter of a mile from their campsite when Storkerson turned his binoculars back toward camp, where the dogs were tied. "Bear!" he exclaimed.

Downwind from the dogs and partially hidden behind a small ridge of ice, a polar bear was stalking. With its neck and snout down in the snow and its rump in the air, the bear had flattened its body against the surface of the ice and was sliding tobogganlike toward the dogs. When it came, the attack would be swift.

Stefansson, who was nearest to the camp, raced with his gun toward the scene. He arrived within firing range just as the great bruin reached Bones. The first shot injured the bear but did not kill it. Enraged, the bear turned on Stefansson, and the man barely had time to fire again before the enormous claws could tear into him. The shot was good, and the bear collapsed "so near that his blood spattered my boots," as Stefansson described it.

By early May, the seals and then the belugas were providing the explorers with food and fuel. The sea animals had arrived just in time, for by that point the men had used up nearly all their supplies. After their kerosene ran out, they cooked by burning the hair from the bear skins they carried as blankets. The blankets and several pairs of worn-out bear-skin boots were fed to the dogs. The skins had little nourishment, but the dogs chewed them hungrily.

The appearance of the seals and whales proved to Stefansson that this great frozen northern sea had more than enough resources to supply exploration parties with food and fuel, so they could survive without carrying huge loads of supplies. The only thing that worried him now was getting from the ice floe to land. For days, their floe remained far offshore, surrounded by open water. Finally, on June 5, winds pushed the floe closer to the shore ice that connected to land. To reach it, they needed to cross one last mile-wide lead. They would have to move quickly, though—the wind and currents could change direction again at any time, taking them so far from shore that they would never make it back to solid ground.

Stefansson had designed his sled so that the runners could be removed and it could be used as a small boat. As the men hurried to prepare the sled, the wind picked up. They watched anxiously as the wind increased to gale force. The water between them and the shore was whipped into a froth.

Bones and the other dogs were loaded into the sled-boat. They were not good sailors. Frightened by the rough seas, they huddled together on one side, trying to get away from the salt spray. The lopsided boat nearly capsized as the men and dogs made their way across the choppy lead. At last, they made it to shore.

For the next three weeks, the dogs pulled the sled through the soft, thawing snow that covered the shore ice. Sometimes the sled sank so deep into drifts that both men and dogs had to pull to free it. They were moving closer and closer to their destination, Banks Island, but for most of June, they remained on pure ice.

Then, on June 22, the men saw a pink glow in the distance. At first Stefansson was puzzled. As they continued ahead, he realized that the pink color was caused by a microscopic plant that grew on snowdrifts only on land. Now Stefansson knew they were almost past the ice cap. When they reached the shore, Bones didn't know that he was on land rather than on floating ice. The ice that covered the barren coastline looked no different from the sea ice he was used to.

By the time they arrived on Banks Island, ninety-six days after the start of their journey, the Stefansson expedition had traveled an estimated 700

Sled dog team pulling through water during spring melt, circa 1910s
—Courtesy Alaska State Library, Dr. Daniel S. Neuman Photograph Collection, P307-0111

miles on moving ice floes. They had completed the trip with no loss of either men or dogs. Stefansson felt they had proved that the Arctic ice caps were "friendly," that is, capable of supporting life. Stefansson was proud that the dogs were in better condition at the end of the voyage than at the beginning. "All our dogs were as fat as it is good for a dog to be," he observed. "But Bones was fatter than that. Perhaps this was his trouble."

Stefansson later wrote of his historic ice floe expedition in a book entitled *The Friendly Arctic*. In it, Stefansson paid special tribute to the dogs on his sled team:

> They have probably done better work than any team in Arctic exploration. Two hundred and forty-four pounds to the dog is, I believe, a heavier load than dogs have heretofore hauled and ours came near making thirty miles a day with that load in fair going. We have never had to do more than help them over the worst places. An Arctic traveler's feeling of gratitude to the dogs can be scarcely less keen than to men.

Dynamite and the Reindeer Fair

HE YUPIK ESKIMO CHILDREN heard the bells first. They were faint and tinkly, coming on January winds from the Bering Sea off the coast of western Alaska. "The *dundit!*" the boys and girls exclaimed, using the Yupik word for reindeer.

It was the sound the children had been waiting for days to hear. They ran from the schoolhouse, in the small village of Igloo (also known as Mary's Igloo) on the Seward Peninsula, and there, on the horizon, they could see the branched antlers of the reindeer. The deer and their drivers were coming for the 1915 reindeer fair, the first ever to be held in Alaska. The fair would take place at the hot springs on the Pilgrim River, a few miles from Igloo, which was the winter home for these Yupik children and their families.

Soon the children could see eight deer, each pulling a single sled. The men on the sleds included Tautuk, the chief herder of the government reindeer herd in Nome, on the seacoast; his brother, Amuktoolik; Carl Lomen, the white man whose reindeer herds contained more than a thousand animals; Walter Shields, superintendent of the schools on the Seward Peninsula, who had organized the fair; and several of their friends. Behind the last sled was tied a particularly beautiful reindeer, with small bells attached to his scarlet neckband. His name was Dynamite. He belonged to the chief herder, Tautuk, who believed that Dynamite was the fastest of all the hundreds of reindeer in western Alaska. Tautuk was sure that in the great sled race, which would be the climax of the reindeer fair, he could drive Dynamite to win.

The children and their teacher, Mr. Hunnicutt, ran to greet the visitors. "Come to the schoolhouse," said Mr. Hunnicutt. "My wife has saved our Christmas turkey for this great occasion."

The men unharnessed the reindeer and tied them to some sturdy black-top grass, which grew higher than the snowpack. The animals used their broad hooves to uncover the grayish white lichens, called reindeer moss, that formed their winter diet. In the summer, the deer grazed on tender young grass, mushrooms, and berries on the peninsula's rolling hills.

Tautuk unhitched Dynamite and paraded him before the children. The animal's ears were clipped in a special way. Herders marked their reindeer's ears to show which ones were theirs. "He's a fleet racer," Tautuk said. "He is faster than any I have ever cared for."

The children admired the beautiful animal. He was a descendent of the Tunguse reindeer that had been brought to Alaska from the coast of Russia's Okhotsk Sea. Although reindeer are closely related to Alaskan caribou, none had lived in this part of North America until the 1890s. By then, whaling ships had depleted western Alaska's population of whales, which

were a major food source for the Eskimos there. The United States government brought in reindeer as a new source of meat. Some of the early reindeer came from Norway and were accompanied by Laplandian herders, who
taught the native Alaskans how to raise them. Many of the Laplanders settled
in Alaska permanently; some of them would be taking part in the fair.

Dynamite was only four and a half feet tall, but his body was long and
he weighed more than 300 pounds. Every inch of his frame was packed
with layers of fat, fuel for the long winter. His coat was a pale brown, but it
would be a deep chocolate in the summer. His thick, tufted coat protected
him from the bitterly cold winds near the Arctic. His antlers seemed even
larger than his body. He would shed them late in the spring, but now, in
their full winter's growth, they branched into brown and white tines, nearly
sixty in all.

Dynamite, like all reindeer, was shortsighted, but his sense of smell was
excellent. He could smell danger when a wolf or a bear moved near. He
could smell the reindeer moss that lay beneath the snow, telling him where
to dig to find it. His hooves were sharp enough to fork out the moss, but
broad enough to support him on snow or boggy tundra.

Throughout the day, more reindeer were brought in, and more guests
arrived, too. Tautuk and Dynamite had come from Nome, a hundred miles
away, which was a five-day journey. Other herders came from places even
farther away, such as Deering and Shishmaref. By evening, more than a
hundred people had gathered to eat the Christmas turkey and reindeer stew.
The Yupik liked their stew meat dipped in seal oil.

When the meal was over, Walter Shields, the school superintendent, told
the guests about the upcoming activities. He explained that the people of Igloo
had prepared a campsite at the fairgrounds with huts for everyone. "They have
wood and stoves ready," Shields said. "They have staked out race trails. We'll

have contests so you can show your skills as herders. We'll show you ways to care for reindeer. We'll share ideas on how to increase the size of the herds."

Then the children sang a song they had made up for the fair. It began, "Hurrah, hurrah, the reindeer men are we!" The guests laughed and clapped and joined in the singing. But soon it grew late. Many of the guests unrolled their deerskins on the schoolhouse floor for the night, but some of the herders, like the Laplander Andrew Bahr, chose to sleep outside. "A house smothers a man once he has the smell and look and feel of the tundra in his blood," Bahr said. "A man with a roof over his head and four walls shutting him in cannot see the sky or feel the wind or even know the time of night by looking overhead."

The next morning, the reindeer were rounded up, harnessed, hitched to sleds, and driven to the fairgrounds. There were dozens of reindeer pulling sleds, and many more unbroken ones, which would be held in corrals at the fairgrounds.

Mr. Hunnicutt and the Igloo families had built circular huts called *too-boo-ga-roos* around the edge of the fairgrounds for the visitors. They were made from willow branches bent toward the center and tied at the top, tee-pee fashion, then covered with sod. There were *tupkes*, too, round-topped huts made by sticking willow shoots into the hard-packed snow and weaving them together, then stretching canvas over the willow frame. Inside all the huts were small wood-burning stoves.

The next few days were the most exciting time the Yupik children could remember. Each day there was a lassoing contest. Hundreds of reindeer were driven from the corrals onto the fairgrounds, where the villagers and guest families formed a circle around the edges. At the signal, the contestants ran to the center of the herd and lassoed as many bull deer as possible in thirty minutes. Only the ones who had shed their antlers counted. At first the bulls were easy to catch. But after they had been lassoed once and let loose, they became savvy of the lassos and began to run and dodge the herders, creating a riveting show for the audience.

Even more thrilling were the wild-deer-driving contests. Contestants had to enter the herd, rope an unbroken reindeer, harness it, hitch it to a sled, and drive it half a mile up the river and back. Driving the wild deer away from the herd was so difficult that one contestant simply tied his deer onto the sled and pulled the sled himself. Others pulled their deer with ropes. But on the way back, the herders had the opposite problem. Once the sled was turned around at the checkpoint, the deer saw the herd and ran back at breakneck speed—it was all the herders could do to control the sleds. Tautuk, the most skilled of the herdsmen, won most of the contests.

The fair also had contests that didn't involve reindeer. One was a fire-making contest, which old Seecup Seraluk, wearing a wolverine headdress, won. He whirled his fire stick between his old hands, sweat streaming down his wrinkled face. In little more than a minute, sparks lit the tinder around the stick. Titkak of Noatak won the snow-melting contest. In nine minutes and thirty-seven seconds, he whittled his kindling, started a fire, and melted a cupful of snow.

Women displayed their own special skills. Seamstresses showed how they used their arms and hands to measure the spotted skins of reindeer fawns for parkas. The skins were sewn together with thread made from the back sinew of the reindeer. The women trimmed the hoods with wolf and wolverine fur for extra protection around the face. Many of the parkas were decorated with bands of designs made by stitching together tiny bits of different-colored skins and furs. Prizes were awarded for the finest parkas.

When the brief hours of daylight ended and the temperatures dropped far below zero, the herders took turns cooking for the crowd. They simmered

Native Alaskans modeling reindeer-skin coats, 1916 —Courtesy Library of Congress

big kettles of white navy beans, then mashed the beans and mixed them with reindeer meat and fat to form large bean cakes. Women served bread they had baked.

When the bright full moon shone down on the rolling, snow-covered tundra, it was nearly as light as day. By the moonlight, many of the men and older boys played Eskimo football, a game resembling soccer. The ball was made of sealskin and stuffed with reindeer hair. Later, as everyone settled in around the fire, the children listened to the old-timers tell tales or watched Charlie Agoovlook make string pictures, working sinew cord around his fingers to form outlines of the local birds and animals. Sometimes Charlie wove the pictures so fast, one after another, that the children's eyes could hardly follow. The English word for Charlie's game is cat's cradle; the Yupik children called it *i-yi-gah-rok*.

Late at night, as the children were snuggled into their deerskin bedrolls inside the low, round *tupkes* they shared with their families, they could hear the sounds of the reindeer in the corral: the long, deep grunts of the mothers calling their fawns, and the fawns' fragile, high-pitched answers.

On the morning of the last day of the fair, everyone joined in a grand parade, dressed in their finest fur garments. The sleds bore flags and streamers, bright banners against the white landscape. Even the deer wore special finery. Their parade harnesses were trimmed with brightly colored felt and decorated with yarn pompoms, and bells were attached to their embroidered neck bands.

The last event of the fair was the eleven-mile one-deer sled race, the race that Tautuk had brought Dynamite here to win. Already Tautuk had won more events than any other herder—his chest was covered with blue and red ribbons. But his brother Amuktoolik had won nothing. He would have no prize to show when they returned to Nome. As the contestants lined up for the start of the race, Tautuk hesitated. If Amuktoolik were to take his place, he might yet have a ribbon to take home.

"Amuktoolik!" he called. He handed his brother the rein. Then the whistle blew, and the deer and their drivers were off. Just as Tautuk knew he would, Dynamite quickly moved out in front. He and Amuktoolik were far ahead as they sped across the tundra, holding the lead until they became distant specks on the horizon. As the racers moved out of sight, the crowd hooted

Sled race, 1922 Reindeer Fair, Alaska —Courtesy Library of Congress

and stomped their feet impatiently until the sleds reappeared. But when they finally came into view again, Tautuk saw that Dynamite had dropped back. Unless Amuktoolik urged him on, he would not win the race. He could see his brother slapping the single rein across Dynamite's neck. As they drew closer, he could hear Amuktoolik crying out to the deer. Dynamite's wide hooves moved faster. He passed one deer, then another. They were almost to the finish line.

But Dynamite's spurt of speed had not come soon enough. Although he was only seconds behind the others, Dynamite came in fourth, not first.

Tautuk knew that if he had been driving the sled, Dynamite would have won. But he didn't mind. There would be a ribbon for the fourth place. And for Tautuk, seeing his brother's happiness as he pinned a white ribbon proudly to his parka was better than winning first prize.

With the big race over, the fair came to a close. It had been a time of good fellowship and good spirits, and the herders had learned much from one another. Satisfied but sorry to go, the visitors packed up their sleds for the long ride home. After many handshakes and promises to meet again the next January, the herders with their reindeer rode away. The children watched until the last deer disappeared over the horizon.

Carl Lomen and Walter Shields, who had organized the fair, felt it had been a great success. In addition to the enjoyable camaraderie and friendly competition, herders had exchanged ideas about how to handle the reindeer and improve their herds.

Later, in a book he wrote about his experiences in Alaska, Lomen said he thought reindeer were "the most interesting creatures on earth. . . . I found them to be dependable and faithful servants of man. I tried to treat them with intelligence and kindness, and they reciprocated in full."

◇◇◇◇◇◇◇◇◇◇◇◇◇◇◇◇◇◇◇◇◇◇

Two more reindeer fairs were held in Alaska, both just as popular as the first one. But in the winter of 1918–19, an influenza epidemic took the lives of Walter Shields and hundreds of villagers and herders. Over the next several years, reindeer were left unattended, some escaping to join herds of wild caribou. Wolves overran much of the reindeer territory, feeding on the easy prey. No further fairs were held in Igloo. A few were held elsewhere in Alaska during the 1920s, but by the end of the decade, the reindeer industry had all but collapsed.

Margie and the
Cold Bay Pups

WHERE WAS MARGIE?

In May 1932, Father Bernard Hubbard, six other scientists, and their dog team journeyed to Unimak Island, near the southernmost tip of the Alaska Peninsula, to explore the strange, scallop-shaped mountains that Father Hubbard believed were breached volcanoes—volcanoes whose tops were weathering away. Later in the summer, they would make their way west to the uncharted Aghileen Pinnacles, hoping to find out how those spectacular peaks had been formed.

One night, as they made camp, the expedition members discovered that one of the dogs—Margie, who had been part of Father Hubbard's explorations of southwestern Alaska's glaciers and volcanoes for the past five years—was missing, along with four of her puppies. The men who had been walking in front had thought Margie was behind them, while those in the rear thought she was up front. Father Hubbard was annoyed—sneaking away was an old trick of hers. The simplest thing would be to leave her behind—but he knew he could not bear to do that.

Lovable but exasperating, Margie often caused trouble for the expedition. She could be willful and disobedient, but she was also the most beautiful A Father Hubbard had ever seen, "a picture dog if ever there was one, black silky fur, pointed ears, expressive eyes, symmetrical white areas on face, ears, chest, and paws, called Margie the Beautiful in the Yukon." More than that, she had served him faithfully through some tough times. He remembered one exploration in particular as being the reason he kept Margie in spite of the problems she caused. Several years earlier, she had been a member of his Yukon team, mushing for 1,600 miles over the snow and ice of northwestern Alaska. During the journey, the explorer-priest had become ill. He was dizzy and weak. With the last of his strength, he had strapped himself to the sled. Margie had been one of the trusty sled dogs who had led him to safety.

Father Bernard Hubbard was known as "the glacier priest" to the millions of Americans who had heard his lectures and seen his photographs. He had made pioneering flights in small planes, climbed the mountains of the Alaska Peninsula, and identified unknown glaciers and volcanoes. During the winter, he traveled across the United States to show photos and movies of his explorations to raise money for Catholic missions and schools in Alaska. Often accompanying him on his lecture tours were his four dogs: Katmai, Mageik, Wolf, and Margie. He once humorously likened them to actors, "a perfect quartet comprising characters for all the heavy parts—a dark villain, a dashing hero, an intriguing heroine, and a funny clown."

Fr. Bernard Hubbard with dogs Mageik and Margie at Yakutat Bay, Alaska, 1936
—Courtesy Santa Clara University Archives

On the previous summer's exploration, Hubbard had planned to take all four of the dogs, "but my beautiful swing dog Margie had to go and have pups in April. So she was forced to stay in the hills of Santa Clara Valley to take care of her family, while with sad eyes she watched Katmai, her life companion on Yukon trails, depart for the Far North. . . . But this year she was presumably free of domestic obligations so along she came." Little did Father Hubbard know that Margie would not be "free of domestic obligations" for very long.

At the start of this expedition, the explorers had crossed miles of rolling tundra to their first campsite. Early one morning, a strange noise had awakened the men. They listened intently, thinking it might be a bear. The sounds, they discovered, were coming from the little shelter where Margie slept. They hurried to investigate, and there, whimpering beneath Margie's thick coat, were seven newborn puppies.

"What can we do with them?" a dismayed Father Hubbard wondered. "A volcano is hardly the proper place for puppies." The team was preparing to leave for a hundred-mile journey, on which each man would be carrying a one-hundred-pound pack. How could they possibly take along seven help-less little puppies? The men considered getting rid of them. Under the cir-cumstances, it would have been the sensible thing to do. But no one wanted the job of executioner. Finally, one of the scientists, Ken Chisholm, said with a shrug, "Well, fellows, let's see if we can bring 'em back alive."

Nick Cavaliere converted the bucket-shaped cover of his camera tripod into a traveling cradle for the newborns, a litter of two males and five fe-males. Ken, who was voted the puppies' caretaker, lined the cradle with soft grass. Margie growled when Ken came to take the pups, but he was firm. As he placed the puppies into their makeshift bed, Margie began to whimper, but Ken softly assured her that her babies would be safe.

Puppies or no puppies, the men continued their work. Carrying the cra-dle in one arm, Ken helped his companions explore the scalloped peaks near the campsite. After completing a nearly month-long study, the team determined that the mountains were indeed the remnants of old volcanoes, just as Father Hubbard had supposed.

By the time the explorers started their journey to the Aghileen Pinnacles, the puppies' eyes were open and they had outgrown the traveling cradle. But they were still too roly-poly to walk far on their own. How were the men going to move them? This time, an empty wooden film box was pressed into service. Ken attached a wire to the box and fastened the other end to

Margie and her pups in their travel box
—Courtesy Santa Clara University Archives

Mageik's harness. Although Mageik, the noble Yukon sled dog, didn't like pulling a baby carriage, Ken coaxed him along as Father Hubbard held the box steady with his ice pick. So the trip across the tundra began.

Though bumped and jostled, the pups stayed good-naturedly in their improvised sled, mostly sleeping. Occasionally the box overturned, and the puppies had to be collected and counted and put back in. The system worked well enough for the first several miles, but soon the terrain became rough and veined with rivers. The men needed both their arms free to steady their heavy packs while testing the ground with their ice picks. They couldn't pull the box of puppies across these swift, silty streams. Ed Levin wondered aloud how they had let themselves get into this predicament.

Mathematics finally solved the problem. There were seven men and seven puppies. Each man could take a pup buttoned inside his shirt as they crossed the river. So that's what they did, and soon Margie's babies were safely across the first stream. Now it was Katmai's turn to baby-sit. The men emptied the packsacks that Katmai carried on his broad back and transferred his load to Mageik, then they stuffed the puppies into Katmai's pack. The proud Katmai hated being a nursemaid even more than Mageik had, but he endured the indignity. The pups, however, were not so stoic. Too cramped, they yelped and whined and wriggled out of the pack. The men had to wrestle with the babies to hold them down and strap them in.

As the party traveled on, the puppies kept crying. Their wailing was so loud and constant that it began to upset Katmai. When the explorers reached the next river, Katmai suddenly jumped into the water, puppies and all. Quickly, Ken slipped off his pack, waded into the chest-deep water, and snagged both Katmai and the pack of howling babies. Father Hubbard helped him pull the animals back to shore.

The men pulled the puppies out of the pack and let Margie lick them dry. "They're sorry-looking little bundles of wet fur, but they seem none the worse for their scare," Father Hubbard said with relief. In fact, the dunking may have done the little rascals some good—they didn't make much noise for the rest of the trip.

After three days of hiking, the explorers set up camp near the Aghileen Pinnacles. Margie's puppies were happy to be free of the packsacks. Awakening when the sun rose, they became the alarm clocks for the expedition. They chased each other around the tents, bumping against the sides where the men's heads lay. "They ought to know we want to sleep!" Ed grumbled.

By this time, the puppies knew the names the explorers had given them. The largest one, who was nearly twice as big as any of his siblings, was called Frosty. He usually ate not only his own food but whatever he could steal from the other pups. Chignik, nicknamed Sour Face, looked like he was frowning. The prettiest pup was Pavlof, her ears sharp and pointed, her tail tipped with white. Unimak was the sweet and quiet one. Kukuk and Adak, according to Father Hubbard, were "just dogs." Then there was Atka, the runt, the one the men had feared was too small to survive. She turned out to be the outstanding puppy of the seven. Strong and wiry, she was the leader of the litter.

For the next five weeks, the explorers examined the steep pinnacles, working their way up icy cliffs and volcanic rock. When at last they reached the summit, Father Hubbard wrote, "All we could do was stare and gasp." They had discovered one of the largest volcanic craters in the world. The top of the peak had been blown to pieces millennia before—all that was left were the vent and some smaller volcanic cones. The explorers now had proof that the Aghileen Pinnacles had once been part of a single great volcano.

Their mission completed, the men prepared to return to the coast, where a boat would be waiting for them. But now the puppies were too big for Katmai to carry alone. The explorers put the three largest pups into Katmai's packs, and the four smaller ones went into packsacks on Margie's back." The puppies strenuously objected to leaving camp, while Katmai and Margie objected just as strenuously to carrying them. But eventually the men and dogs were on their way.

They were only a day's journey from the coast when the explorers discovered that Margie and her load of pups were missing. She had apparently slipped away and hidden, as she had a bad habit of doing. But the realization that the puppies were gone distressed the men, especially Father Hubbard.

"We and the puppies had survived bears and flood and starvation," he wrote in his journal. "Yet here, in good weather, this disaster threatened an end to our bringing all seven back alive."

It was too late to look for Margie that night. Father Hubbard couldn't sleep thinking of the beautiful malamute and the four little pups strapped on her back. He wondered whether she was lost in the swamps or had gotten swept away in one of the rivers they had crossed that day. They might be able to find her in the daylight, but could the expedition spare the time to look for a few dogs?

The men knew Father Hubbard hoped to use the pups in future lectures, and he wanted to show that despite five months of difficult exploration, they had successfully cared for seven helpless puppies. The next morning after breakfast, Ed and Ken approached Father Hubbard. "We know how you feel about the puppies, Father," Ken said, "so Ed and I are going to look for them." Taking Wolf with them, the two scientists retraced the previous day's trail across the marshes, slogging through dense tangles of alders.

Father Hubbard waited at camp. He knew the chances of finding the dogs alive was slim. Evening came; the wind rose and rain fell. He had nearly given up hope when he saw Ken and Ed appear. With them was Wolf. And—yes, there was another dog! They'd found Margie! As they came into camp, Father Hubbard saw that Wolf was wearing Margie's pack, and inside were all four puppies. "You can't kill malamutes," Ed remarked. "They're too tough."

Over cups of hot chocolate, the searchers told their story. They had discovered Atka, the runt, first. She'd been paddling around in the middle of a swamp. It was almost an hour before they found Margie and the other three puppies, still in the packsacks. "She knew she'd done something wrong," Ed said. "The minute she saw us she tried to run away again. We chased and caught her, and what do you think? She bit me on the arm!"

"And that wasn't all, either," Ken added. "Margie wouldn't come along, and she wouldn't pack the puppies. So we gave the pups to Wolf while we pulled Margie along with a rope. She ought to be shot!"

Father Hubbard said he didn't blame Ken for feeling that way. But inside, he was overjoyed that Margie was safe and sound. Even though she could be unruly, stubborn, and downright ornery, she was precious to him.

Father Hubbard's love for Margie would be tested once more later that summer. While the pups frolicked on the deck of the expedition's ship in Katmai Bay, the men and their dogs explored the hot pools and desolate landscape of the Valley of Ten Thousand Smokes. During a violent storm, as the explorers struggled through the pass out of the valley, Margie disappeared. Risking his own life, Father Hubbard searched for her. He had nearly given up hope when through the wind he heard a whine. He found her lying wet, shivering, and weak at the bottom of a gully. He helped her up, coaxed her from the gully and onto the trail, and led her gently out of the storm and back to camp.

Many years later, Father Hubbard expressed how he felt about his dogs:

> With all their shortcomings, we love our dogs and we accept them the way they are. They have been our constant and faithful companions. They have gone where we have gone, suffered hunger and wet and cold when we have and have sometimes risen to astonishing heights of heroism. I think that Almighty God has given us dogs to teach us fidelity. When their own instinct has told them they were going into danger, they have followed because we have led. You can be cruel to a dog, punish him without cause—but make the least sign of recognition and he forgives all. It takes an exceptionally good man to do this. A dog does more: he not only forgives instantly, but he also forgets.

More True Stories of the Alaska Frontier

"Klondike Mike" Mahoney was one of the first mail carriers in Alaska. Along with supplies, he provided word-of-mouth news to miners along the creeks of interior Alaska and the Yukon during the Klondike gold rush of the late 1890s. He was sometimes called the "walking newspaper" of the goldfields. He carried outgoing mail from Dawson to Skagway by dog team. The trip took a month and required 500 pounds of food and supplies for Mike and his dogs. He eventually struck it rich in the goldfields, but he never stopped working. For his toughness and his storytelling, Klondike Mike became a northern legend.

<><><><><><><><><><><><><><><>

The first native Alaskan woman to own her own reindeer herd was Changunak, also called Sinrock Mary, after the Inupiat settlement where she lived, near Nome. Reindeer helped make her the richest woman in Alaska in the early 1900s and earned her the title the "Reindeer Queen." When fresh food was scarce, Mary sold reindeer meat to area gold miners, the army at Fort St. Michael, and local merchants. She was noted for her determination, her skill with the animals, and her generosity.

<><><><><><><><><><><><><><><>

Until airplanes allowed access to hospitals from remote parts of Alaska, emergency medical treatment in winter depended on the speed and skill of mushers and their dog teams. Perhaps the most famous Alaska medical emergency, during the Nome diphtheria epidemic of 1925, became known as the "Great Race of Mercy," also called the "race against death."

Dozens of children around Nome were sick and dying of diphtheria, an infectious disease that damages the heart and nervous system. Hundreds of children and adults were in danger of becoming infected. Without the antitoxin serum, the mortality rate for diphtheria was almost 100 percent. But the nearest available serum was hundreds of miles away in Anchorage. The only way to get the medicine to Nome was by dogsled. Mushers living along the remote cross-country trails received word of the emergency by radio.

The serum was placed aboard the Alaska Railroad at Anchorage and carried to Nenana, southwest of Fairbanks. There it was carefully wrapped in furs to prevent it from freezing before being strapped onto sleds. The first driver and his dogs took off to meet the next musher, fifty miles away. Twenty mushers and some 150 dogs ran in turn around the clock in gale force winds and temperatures that dropped far below zero. The teams carried the antitoxin 674 miles in 127 hours. When the serum arrived in Nome, not a single vial had been broken. Within 24 hours, the epidemic was under control.

Norwegian Gunnar Kaasen was the final musher in the relay. His lead dog, Balto, gained nationwide fame, and Balto's statue still stands in New York City's Central Park. However, another Norwegian, Leonhard Seppala, and his team, led by a Siberian huskie named Togo, were recognized for mushing the longest distance over the most hazardous part of the trail.

The heroic serum run is honored at Alaska's annual Iditarod dog sled race. One respected musher is selected as the Leonhard Seppala Honorary Musher, who starts the race. At the Iditarod and in history, Seppala, along with the nineteen other mushers and their dogs, will always be remembered for winning the 1925 "race against death."

◇◇◇◇◇◇◇◇◇◇◇◇◇◇◇◇◇◇◇◇◇◇◇◇

By the 1930s, aviation had come to Alaska, and bush pilots were flying to many Alaskan villages. One of the most colorful of these fliers was Archie

Ferguson, who established air service to Kotzebue in 1931. He set high standards for the pilots he hired, but he himself was not very good at flying. On one occasion, Ferguson radioed that a bear he was transporting had broken loose and was in the cockpit with him. When his Cessna touched down smoothly in Kotzebue, onlookers said it was the best landing Archie Ferguson had ever made. Rumor had it that the bear had taken over the controls.

Places to Visit

STICKEEN

SOUTHEASTERN ALASKA/GLACIER BAY

- Glacier Bay National Park and Preserve. In this 5,000-square-mile wilderness park, visitors can see the towering tidewater glaciers that John Muir explored, including one named for Muir himself. The main visitor center is in the Glacier Bay Lodge at Bartlett Cove. The Glacier Bay Preserve Office and Visitor Center is in the village of Yakutat. The only way to access the bay itself is by air or water. Cruise ships and tour boats are the most popular means of viewing the spectacular glaciers.

JOHN MUIR

- Fort William H. Seward National Historic Landmark, Haines. John Muir Center is in Chilkat Eagle B&B Inn, located in the fort's historic district.

- John Muir National Historic Site, Martinez, California. Naturalist John Muir is honored not just in Alaska, but around the world. There is even a John Muir Museum in Scotland, Muir's homeland. The museum at the National Historic Site in California, originally the Muir family's home, is managed by the National Park Service.

TLINGIT CULTURE

- Alaska Indian Arts, Haines. Interpretive talks on Tlingit culture and area history; totem-pole carving.

- Chief Shakes Tribal House, Wrangell. A pile-supported walkway leads to Shakes Island, in the middle of Wrangell Harbor, where visitors can see Tlingit totems and a replica of a Tlingit tribal house built by the Civilian Conservation Corps.

- Clausen Memorial Museum, Petersburg. Tlingit artifacts as well as local history.

- Sheldon Museum and Cultural Center, Haines. Tlingit artifacts and cultural displays. Area pioneer and Fort Seward history. Also John Muir–related items.

- Sitka Historical Society Museum, Sitka. Area's Russian and American history and Tlingit culture.

- Sitka National Historical Park, Sitka. Area history. Visitor center maintains Southeast Alaska Indian Cultural Center.

- Totem Bight State Historical Park, Ketchikan. Displays CCC-built replicas of native buildings and totem art.

- Totem Heritage Center, Ketchikan. Preserves Tligit totem poles.

- Wrangell Museum, Wrangell. Local history, including Tligit history and culture.

DINNAJI

CENTRAL/INTERIOR ALASKA/DENALI

- Big Delta State Historical Park. Museum site includes indoor and outdoor displays of the region's history.

- Denali National Park and Preserve. Visitors can travel its one road by park bus for spectacular views of Mt. McKinley. On the way, you may see Dall sheep, wolves, grizzly bears, moose, or caribou. It is the only national park to have sled dogs that help protect its wildlife. You can visit the kennels to meet the dogs and learn more about their history.

- Talkeetna Historical Society Museum, Talkeetna. Has info on area history, mountain climbing, and Mt. McKinley.

ATHAPASKAN CULTURE

- Alfred Starr Nenana Cultural Center, Nenana. Athapaskan artifacts and culture, as well as regional and dog-mushing history.

JUDGE WICKERSHAM

- Eagle Historic District, Eagle. Walking tour includes Judge Wickersham's courthouse.

- Wickersham House Museum, Fairbanks. The house, built by Judge Wickersham himself, is a re-creation of early life in Fairbanks.

- Wickersham State Historic Site, Juneau. Former Wickersham home holds large collection of Wickersham materials and historic artifacts.

BONES

FAR NORTHERN ALASKA/ARCTIC

- Arctic National Wildlife Refuge. A remote and rugged land reserve managed by the U.S. Fish and Wildlife Service. Visitors are cautioned that the refuge is wild country; unguided visits require careful planning and backcountry experience.

- Inupiat Native Heritage Center, Barrow. Barrow is in the northernmost part of Alaska, not far from where Stefansson began his ice-floe journey. The center displays the history of the Inupiat people and their traditional hunting of bowhead whales. Affiliated with the New Bedford Whaling National Historic Park, it tells the story of commercial whaling in the Arctic.

- Nana Museum of the Arctic, Kotzebue. Arctic natural history and Eskimo culture.

STEFANSSON

- American Museum of Natural History, New York, New York. Has extensive materials on Stefansson expeditions.

DYNAMITE

Western Alaska/Seward Peninsula

- Bering Land Bridge National Preserve. The preserve is part of the area near Nome where reindeer herds were once raised. It is a remnant of the land bridge that thousands of years ago once connected what are now Siberia and Alaska. Its headquarters are in Nome, where there is a small interpretative center.

- Carrie McLain Memorial Museum, Nome. History of Seward Peninsula, Nome region. Includes displays on Eskimo culture, Bering Land Bridge, gold rush, and dog mushing.

Yupik Culture

- Samuel K. Fox Museum, Dillingham. Yupik culture and artifacts.
- Yup'iit Piciryarait Library, Museum, and Cultural Center, Bethel.

MARGIE

Southwestern Alaska/Alaska Peninsula/ Aleutian Islands

- Alaska Peninsula National Wildlife Refuge. The pinnacles that Father Hubbard explored form part of the boundary between this refuge and Izembek National Wildlife Refuge (below). The visitor center is at King Salmon, where there are exhibits and interactive programs.

- Izembek National Wildlife Refuge. Headquartered in remote Cold Bay, the refuge has a small observation building overlooking Izembek Lagoon and has 360-degree viewing windows where visitors can look for whales, otters, and waterfowl.

- Museum of the Aleutians, Unalaska. History museum with focus on indigenous culture.

FATHER HUBBARD

- De Saisset Museum, Santa Clara University, Santa Clara, California. Houses large collection of materials related to Father Hubbard.

SLED DOGS

- Denali National Park and Preserve. See under Dinnaji.
- Dog Mushing Museum, Fairbanks. Headquarters of Alaskan Dog Mushers' Association. Displays on dog-mushing history and live dog-sled demonstrations.
- Iditarod National Historic Trail, Nome.

OTHER ALASKA HISTORY, NATURAL HISTORY, AND NATIVE CULTURES

- Alaska Native Heritage Center, Anchorage. Indoor and outdoor exhibits of Alaska's eleven native groups.
- Alaska State Museum, Juneau. A ten-minute walk from the cruise-ship docks in Juneau, the Alaska State Museum includes displays on Alaska's Native American groups, the Russian-American years, and the state's natural resources, as well as an impressive collection of fine art.
- Anchorage Museum at Rasmuson Center (Anchorage Museum of History and Art), Anchorage. Alaska history, art, and native culture.
- Anchorage Museum of Natural History, Anchorage. Includes information about the ice age and polar dinosaurs. Largest collection of rocks, minerals, and fossils in the state.
- Corrington Museum of Alaska History, Skagway.
- Sheldon Jackson Museum, Sitka. Oldest museum in Alaska. Has exceptional collection of native Alaskan material. Exhibits on history and natural history of Alaska.

- University of Alaska Museum of the North, Fairbanks. The only research and teaching museum in Alaska, it includes a gallery that introduces Alaska's five major geographic regions. One room, "the place where you listen," has sound and light displays that include the aurora borealis. Materials on reindeer fair, sled dogs, native Alaskan culture, and more.

WEB SITES

- Alaska Kids' Stuff has history, culture, climate, games, and facts: http://sled.alaska.edu/kids.html
- Denali National Park site includes "For Kids" history, nature, and science: http://www.ns.gov/dena/naturescience/index.html

Selected Bibliography

Andrews, C. L. *The Eskimo and His Reindeer in Alaska*. Caldwell, Idaho: Caxton Printers, 1939.

Hubbard, Bernard R. *Cradle of the Storms*. New York: Dodd, Mead & Co., 1935.

Lomen, Carl J. *Fifty Years in Alaska*. New York: David McKay Co., 1954.

Muir, John. *Travels in Alaska*. Boston: Houghton-Mifflin, 1915.

Murphy, Claire Rudolf, and Jane G. Haigh. *Gold Rush Women*. Portland, Oregon: Alaska Northwest Books, 1997.

Potter, Jean. *The Flying North*. Indianapolis: Curtis Publishing, 1947.

Salisbury, Gay, and Laney Salisbury. *The Cruelest Miles: The Heroic Story of Dogs and Men in a Race Against an Epidemic*. New York: W. W. Norton, 2003.

Schwalbe, Anna Bixbaum. *Dayspring on the Kuskokwim: The Story of Moravian Missions in Alaska*. Bethlehem, Pennsylvania.: Moravian Press, 1951.

Spurr, Josiah Edward. "The Log of the Kuskokwim, an Exploration in Alaska." Manuscript, 1898. Elmer Ramusson Library, University of Alaska, Fairbanks.

Stefansson, Vilhjalmur. *The Friendly Arctic: The Story of Five Years in Polar Regions*. New York: Macmillan Co., 1944.

Stuck, Hudson. "The Ascent of Denali." In *Denali: Deception, Defeat, and Triumph*. Seattle: Mountaineers Books, 2001.

Wheeler, Keith. *The Alaskans*. Vol. 20, *The Old West*. New York: Time-Life Books, 1977.

Wickersham, James. *Old Yukon: Tales, Trails, Trials*. Washington, D.C.: Washington Law Book Co., 1938.

Young, Samuel Hall. *Alaska Days with John Muir*. Salt Lake City: Peregrine Smith Books, 1991.

Index

Laplanders, 37–38
Levin, Ed, 49, 51
Lomen, Carl, 35, 43

malamutes, 45, 51
McKinley, Mount (Denali), 1, 12–13, 16–19, 22, 23
McLeod, John, 13, 15, 19
Muir, John, 1, 3–10

Nenana, 23

parkas, 39
polar bears, 28, 30

reindeer, 34–43
reindeer moss, 35

seals, 25, 30
Seraluk, Seecup, 39
Seward Peninsula, 34, 35
Shields, Walter, 35, 37, 43
sled dogs, 24–33, 44–52
steamboats, 10, 11, 21, 22
Stefansson, Vilhjalmur, 25–33
Stevens, Mort, 13, 15

Stikine Indians, 10
Stikine River, 10
Storkerson, Storker, 25, 26, 28, 30
Stuck, Hudson, 23

Tanana River, 18, 21, 22
Tanana Valley, 11, 12
Tautuk, 35, 37, 39, 41, 43
Tena Athapaskans, 11–13, 15–18, 22, 23
Titkak, 39
Tlingits, 5, 9, 10
too-boo-ga-roos, 38
tupkes, 38, 41

volcanoes, 44, 45, 47, 50

Webb, Charlie, 13, 15, 18, 21
whales, 25, 30, 35; belugas, 25, 30
Wickersham, James, 1, 12–22

Yako (legend of), 16–18, 22
Yosemite National Park, 10
Young, Rev. S. Hall, 5, 9, 10
Yukon River, 1, 17
Yupiks, 34, 37, 38, 41

ABOUT THE AUTHOR

 Marjorie Cochrane, a former staff writer for newspapers in Alaska and Idaho, holds a journalism degree from the University of Oregon. After retiring, she and her late husband, Byron, spent ten years growing coffee on Hawaii's Kona coast. She now makes her home on Washington's Long Beach peninsula. She has five children and seventeen grandchildren.

Marjorie is the author of *Between Two Rivers*, a community history of Chugiak-Eagle River, where she lived for many years. Her children's stories and feature articles have appeared in numerous publications in the Northwest.

ABOUT THE ILLUSTRATOR

 Jon Van Zyle, one of Alaska's premier artists, is an award-winning painter and children's book illustrator. During his three-decade career, he has received countless honors in the United States, Europe, and Russia, and he has been the official artist of the Iditarod races since 1979. His dozens of children's books include *Jon Van Zyle's Alaska Sketchbook*, winner of a Benjamin Franklin Book Award, and the multiple-award-winning *The Great Serum Race*.

Jon and his wife, Jona, also an artist, live near Eagle River, Alaska, where they raise and train Siberian huskies. Jon's Web site is www.jonvanzyle.com, which features his limited-edition prints, posters, and books, Jona's artwork, and Iditarod merchandise.

We encourage you to patronize your local bookstore. Most stores will order any title they do not stock. You may also order directly from Mountain Press, using the order form provided below or by calling our toll-free, 24-hour number.

Young Adult and Children's titles of interest:

YOUNG ADULT

_____ Bold Women in Michigan's History	paper/$12.00
_____Crazy Horse: A Photographic Biography	paper/$20.00
_____Custer: A Photographic Biography	paper/$24.00
_____Lewis and Clark: A Photographic Journey	paper/$18.00
_____The Oregon Trail: A Photographic Journey	paper/$18.00
_____The Pony Express: A Photographic History	paper/$22.00
_____Sacagawea's Son: The Life of Jean Baptiste Charbonneau	paper/$10.00
_____Smoky: The Cowhorse	paper/$16.00
_____Stories of Young Pioneers: In Their Own Words	paper/$14.00
_____What's So Great About Granite?	paper/$18.00

CHILDREN

_____Awesome Osprey: Fishing Birds of the World	paper/$12.00
_____Blind Tom: The Horse Who Helped Build the Great Railroad	paper/$10.00
_____The Charcoal Forest: How Fire Helps Animals and Plants	paper/$12.00
_____Cowboy in the Making	cloth/$15.00
_____Glacier National Park: An ABC Adventure	paper/$10.00
_____Loons: Diving Birds of the North	paper/$12.00
_____My First Horse	paper/$16.00
_____Nature's Yucky! Gross Stuff That Helps Nature Work	paper/$10.00
_____Nature's Yucky 2! The Desert Southwest	paper/$12.00
_____Owls: Whoo Are They?	paper/$12.00
_____Snowy Owls: Whoo Are They?	cloth/$12.00
_____Spotted Bear: A Rocky Mountain Folktale	cloth/$15.00
_____Three Dogs, Two Mules, and a Reindeer	cloth/$15.00
_____The Will James Cowboy Book	cloth/$18.00
_____You Can Be a Nature Detective	paper/$14.00
_____Young Cowboy	cloth/$15.00

Please include $3.00 per order to cover shipping and handling.

Send the books marked above. I enclose $_____

Name _____

Address _____

City/State/Zip _____

☐ Payment enclosed (check or money order in U.S. funds)

Bill my: ☐VISA ☐MasterCard ☐Discover ☐American Express

Card No._____

Security Code #_____   Expiration Date _____

Signature _____

MOUNTAIN PRESS PUBLISHING COMPANY
P. O. Box 2399 • Missoula, MT 59806 • Fax 406-728-1635
Order Toll Free 1-800-234-5308 • *Have your credit card ready*
E-mail: info@mtnpress.com • Web site: www.mountain-press.com